POLITICS AND GOVERNMENT IN ANCIENT GREECE

MELANIE ANN APEL

The Rosen Publishing Group's

PowerKids Press™
PRIMARY SOURCE

New York

For Lisa and Rob Tolnai. Love, Melanie

Published in 2004 by The Rosen Publishing Group, Inc.
29 East 21st Street, New York, NY 10010

First Edition

Editor: Joanne Randolph
Book Design: Michael DeGuzman
Layout Design: Kim Sonsky
Photo Researcher: Peter Tomlinson

Photo Credits: Cover (center) AKG London/Peter Connolly; cover (right) The Art Archive/JFB; p. 4 Library of Congress, Geography and Map Division; p. 4 (inset) photography by Maria Daniels, courtesy of the Perseus Digital Library Project; pp. 7 (center), 16 (bottom) AKG London/John Hios; pp. 7 (inset), 19 Erich Lessing/Art Resource, NY; pp. 8, 12 (right), 16 (top) The Art Archive/Agora Museum Athens/Dagli Orti; p. 11 Scala/Art Resource, NY; p. 12 (center) © Vanni Archive/CORBIS; p. 15 The Art Archive/Dagli Orti; p. 20 (top) The Art Archive/Archaeological Museum Naples/Dagli Orti; p. 20 (bottom) © Eric and David Hosking/CORBIS.

Apel, Melanie Ann.
Politics and government in ancient Greece / Melanie Ann Apel.—1st ed.
      v. cm.— (Primary sources of ancient civilizations. Greece)
Includes bibliographical references and index.
Contents: An ever-changing government—Most famous oligarchy: Sparta—Tyranny—Solon takes over—Democracy rules—The assembly—In the court of law—The military—Athens and Sparta at odds—The men who ruled the land.
   ISBN 0-8239-6771-9 (library binding)—ISBN 0-8239-8939-9 (paperback)
1. Greece—Politics and government—To 146 B.C.—Juvenile literature. [1. Greece—Politics and government—To 146 B.C.] I. Title. II. Series.
   JC73 .A59 2004
   320.938—dc21
                                                                                    2003000747

Manufactured in the United States of America

Contents

An Ever-Changing Government   5

The Most Famous Oligarchy   6

Tyranny   9

Solon and Athens   10

Democracy Rules   13

The Assembly   14

In the Court of Law   17

The Military   18

Athens and Sparta at Odds   21

The Men Who Ruled the Land   22

Glossary   23

Index   24

Primary Sources   24

Web Sites   24

People in Greek city-states built forts to protect themselves from attack. Here are ruins of Eleutherai, one of several forts that surrounded Athens.

GRAECIAE
VNIVERSAE
SECVNDVM
HODIERNVM
SITVM NEO
TERICA DE
SCRIPTIO.

4

An Ever-Changing Government

Government was an important yet steadily changing part of life in ancient Greece. Ancient Greece was made up of many small areas, all separated from one another by mountains or water. These areas were called city-states and were almost like small, independent countries. Each city-state had at least one large fort, built so that the people could defend themselves from enemies. Every city-state had its own government, an army, and its own currency. Around 700 B.C., most city-states, including Sparta and Athens, were ruled by an oligarchy. An oligarchy is a system of government in which a small number of rich, powerful men rule a larger group of people.

This is a map of Greece created by Abraham Ortelius between 1527 and 1598 and published in an atlas entitled Theatrum Orbis Terrarum *(The Picture of the World).*

The Most Famous Oligarchy

By 500 B.C., Sparta was the most powerful Greek oligarchy. As a society of warriors, Sparta's two kings were the leaders of the army. They ruled as part of a council of 28 members who were elected by the citizens to serve for one year. There were also five officials called elders who served life terms. The councilmen were the ones who made all the decisions and wrote, passed, and made sure people followed all the laws. They were the ones who really controlled the government. Sparta also had an Assembly, made up of citizens who were expected to approve these laws without debate.

Spartan king Leonidas is shown at Thermopylae. He died in battle with 300 fellow Spartans at Thermopylae in 480 B.C. ▶

The Gortyn Code, found carved on a wall in Crete, is one of the most important examples of ancient Greek law. These laws date from the 400s B.C.

8

Tyranny

Because an oligarchy gives power to a small group of people, this type of government was not popular with the Greek people. It allowed aristocrats to become wealthier by taking land and money away from poor farmers. The people rebelled against the government. To restore order after these revolts, tyrants often took control of the government by force. Tyrants could be very hard on the people, taking away land or forcing people to leave their homes. Tyrants often had many enemies among their citizens because of the way they treated people. Eventually tyrants were thrown out of office, too, and oligarchies came back. Finally democracy was adopted.

Greeks could ostracize, or send away, a politician who they believed would become a tyrant. They gave this person an ostracon, such as this one that bears the name Themistocles. Under their democracy, there was a law that stated that anyone who killed a tyrant would not be punished.

Solon and Athens

Until the seventh century B.C., Athens had been ruled by kings, oligarchies, or tyrants. These rulers made all the decisions, many of which were not good for the people. For example, farmers could be sold as slaves if they did not have a good harvest and could not pay their loans. Around 594 B.C., the Athenians decided that they wanted a voice in government. They elected a man named Solon to rule. Together, Solon and the people tried a new form of government called a democracy. After Solon's death, tyrants again controlled Athens. In 507 B.C., Cleisthenes came to power. He gave all citizens the right to vote, freedom of speech, and many other new rights. The Athenian government was officially a democracy.

Solon helped the farmers by clearing all their debts and freeing farmers who had been sold into slavery.

ΣΟΛΩΝ

ΟΝΟΜΟΘΕΤΗΣ

Right: *This is the lottery, or allotment, machine, called the kleroterion. The Athenians used this machine to choose their officials.*

Democracy Rules

Democracy, or government by the people, exists today. It gets its name from the Greek words for people, *demos*, and rule, *kratos*. Following the example set by Athens, many other city-states in ancient Greece changed their governments to democracies. Only the freemen, or those who were not owned as slaves and had been born in Greece, were considered citizens in ancient Greece. As citizens, men had privileges. Citizens elected high-ranking officials, such as judges and generals. Each year, citizens were selected to fill no fewer than 600 government positions through a system called a lottery. These positions ranged from treasurers to prison guards. Citizens could speak in court, own land, and serve in the army.

◀ *Pericles, one of the leaders in Athens who helped to establish democracy, had the Parthenon, a temple to Athena, built to stand for Athenian culture.*

The Assembly

About 40 times each year men would go to the Assembly at the agora. The Assembly in Athens met on a hill and was often attended by thousands of citizens. Men went to the Assembly to talk about governmental matters. The Assembly met early in the morning and often lasted until well after dark. With so many people in attendance, discussions could take a long time and people became emotional over the way they thought things should be done. Nonetheless, debates over issues usually resulted in fair decisions. When the Assembly was not in session, the city-state was run by a group of citizens who had been elected or chosen by lottery.

The agora served as the town hall and a general meeting place in which Greek men could discuss ideas. Pictured are the ruins of the ▶ *upper agora located in Ephesus, in present-day Turkey.*

15

A water clock, called a clepsydra, was used to measure the length of the speeches given in the Greek courts. To keep trials moving, the accused could only speak for as long as it took water to run from one pottery bowl into another.

Men carried a ticket made from clay to identify themselves as jurors.

In the Court of Law

All people in ancient Greece were expected to obey the laws. Citizens made up the juries for trials, much as they do today in the United States. Six thousand jurors were chosen by lottery from the many citizens who volunteered to serve each year. Each juror was selected to serve for a period of one year. A juror would serve on as many juries as needed during that year. When a juror was selected, he received a stone ticket bearing his name. Jurors needed these tickets to enter court. At the end of each trial, each juror was given payment for serving as a juror. For each trial, at least 200 jurors were chosen by lottery to attend. At a trial's conclusion, each juror dropped a special ballot into a box to vote on whether the accused person was innocent or guilty.

The Military

Part of the government's job was to defend the city-state against other city-states and armies from foreign lands. The soldiers of Sparta took their work so seriously that, at the age of seven, boys left their homes and moved to military schools to train for their lives in the military. The rest of ancient Greece was different. Although there was no full-time army, each city-state required all freeborn men over age 20 and under age 60 to serve as part-time soldiers. During times of war, all citizens became active soldiers. These men were required to provide their own weapons and armor. Most of the men fought as foot soldiers, called hoplites. Some city-states also had navies with warships.

Greek soldiers wore helmets, such as this bronze one from the sixth century B.C., which covered the entire head and most of the face. ▶

Above: Greek soldiers wore armor that was usually made from bronze or animal hide. In one hand a soldier held a round metal shield for protection. The shield was often decorated with pictures. This soldier carries a spear. Others used swords or bows and arrows.

19

Right: *Shown is the tomb, or grave, of nearly 200 Greek soldiers who died during the Battle of Marathon. The Athenians sent a runner to Athens to share the news of their victory. This man's run from Marathon is what gave the present-day marathon its name.*

Athens and Sparta at Odds

Athens and Sparta emerged as ancient Greece's two most powerful city-states. Athens and Sparta were enemies, though, and fought often. The smaller city-states and villages attacked one another, too. Wars were usually fought over land, because people lacked enough food and land on which to plant crops.

Greeks also fought wars against invading armies from outside Greece. For example, in 490 B.C., Persia invaded Greece. The Athenian army faced the Persians on the plains of Marathon, north of Athens. The Athenian army was strong and well trained. They forced the Persian army back to their ships, killing about 6,400 of the Persian men.

◀ Top: *This painting of Greek hoplites shows how the Greek army fought using a phalanx. This meant they stood so that their shields formed a wall, or phalanx, against enemy attack.*

The Men Who Ruled the Land

Throughout ancient Greek history, many great men helped to shape the civilization that we remember and study today. Some of these men were kings, such as Alexander the Great, who ruled during the third century B.C. He built a huge empire and became well known for working to spread the culture of ancient Greece abroad. Other men, such as Solon, were elected officials. In Athens in the 400s B.C., a man named Pericles was elected chief magistrate nearly every year for about 30 years. Pericles helped to make Athens the strongest city-state in ancient Greece. Each of these men left their mark on Greece and on history, paving the way for ideas, such as democracy and the jury system, that are still in use today.

Glossary

aristocrats (uh-RIS-tuh-krats) Members of the wealthy upper class.

ballot (BA-lut) An object used in voting.

council (KOWN-sul) A group called together to discuss or settle questions.

culture (KUL-chur) The beliefs, practices, and arts of a group of people.

debate (dih-BAYT) To argue or discuss.

defend (dih-FEND) To guard from harm.

democracy (dih-MAH-kruh-see) A government that is run by the people who live under it.

empire (EM-pyr) A large area controlled by one ruler.

invading (in-VAYD-ing) Entering a place in order to attack and take over.

lottery (LAH-tuh-ree) A drawing of lots used to decide something. Lots are objects used as counters in a lottery.

magistrate (MA-jih-strayt) An official who makes sure that laws are obeyed.

oligarchy (AH-lih-gar-kee) A system of government in which a small number of people hold the power over the larger group.

privileges (PRIV-lij-ez) Special rights or favors.

rebelled (rih-BELD) Disobeyed the people or the country in charge.

restore (rih-STOR) Put back, return to an earlier state.

revolts (ri-VOLTS) Fights against the authority of a government.

tyrants (TY-rints) A ruler who uses power to be cruel to others.

Index

A
army(ies), 13, 18, 21
Assembly, 6, 14
Athens, Greece, 5, 10,
    13–14, 21–22

C
city-state(s), 5, 13–14,
    18, 21–22
Cleisthenes, 10

D
debates, 14
democracy, 9–10, 13,
    22

F
farmers, 9–10

J
juries, 17

L
laws, 6, 17
lottery, 13–14

M
Marathon, Greece, 21

O
oligarchy(ies), 5–6,
    9–10

S
slaves, 10, 13
Solon, 10, 22
Sparta, Greece, 5–6,
    18, 21

T
trial(s), 17
tyrants, 9–10

Primary Sources

Cover. A fifth-century-B.C. vase painting of Greek hoplites, or infantrymen, putting on their armor. **Inset.** Bust of Pericles. Stone. Fifth century B.C. From the Greek School. Held at the Vatican Museums and Galleries. Vatican City, Italy. **Page 4. Inset.** Eleutherai Fortress. Photograph of Tower 5 on North Wall, facing west. **Page 7. Inset.** The Gortyn Code. Carved into a wall in Crete, which now forms part of the Roman Odeon. 400s B.C. These laws are a fundamental legal text of ancient Greece. **Page 8.** Ostracon with the name Themistocles carved into it. Terracotta potsherd. Fifth century B.C. Agora Museum. Athens, Greece. **Page 11.** Bust of Solon. Archaic Period. Museo di Andrea del Castagno. Uffizi. Florence, Italy. **Page 12.** Cella of the Parthenon. Built by Phidias in 447–438 B.C. Athens, Greece. **Inset.** Kleroterion. The allotment machine Athenians used to select their legislators. Classical Greek Period. Agora Museum. Athens, Greece. **Page 15.** Upper agora showing ionic capitals on the columns, with bull's head design. Ephesus, Turkey (part of Ancient Greece at the time). **Page 16.** A clepsydra, or water clock, used to measure time in Athenian courts of justice. Fifth century B.C. Found in the agora of Athens, Greece. Agora Museum. Athens, Greece. **Bottom.** Clay tablet used as identification card for jurors. Agora Museum. Athens, Greece. **Page 19.** Bronze helmet. Corinthian type. Late sixth century B.C. From Tchelopetchene near Sofia. **Inset.** Warrior with shield and spear. Sixth-century-B.C. Greek vase painting. National Archeological Museum. **Page 20.** Running soldiers. Vase detail. Sixth century B.C. Greek. Archaeological Museum. Naples, Italy. **Inset.** Marathon Tomb. The collective tomb of some 190 Greek soldiers, killed in a battle against the Persians on a plain near Marathon, Greece. 490 B.C.

Web Sites

Due to the changing nature of Internet links, PowerKids Press has developed an online list of Web sites related to the subject of this book. This site is updated regularly. Please use this link to access the list:
www.powerkidslinks.com/psaciv/poligre/